Winning Doubles Strategy for Recreational Tennis Players

Tips and Tactics for Transforming Your Game

GERRY DONOHUE

Copyright © 2016 Gerry Donohue
All rights reserved.
ISBN-13: 978-1533430960

Introduction	1
Basic Skills Needed for Strategic Doubles	4
No Unforced Errors	6
Communicate, Communicate, Communicate	8
Keep Moving Forward	11
Protect the Middle of the Court	12
Play the Percentages	13
Control—Not Power	15
Doubles is Won at the Net	17
Importance of Court Positioning	20
Importance of Court Positioning at the Net	22
Poaching	23
Returning Serve	26
Choosing Teams	29
Which Side of the Court	31
Whose Shot Is It?	33
Mixed Doubles Problem	35
Winning the Key Points	36
Two Captains	38
One Up, One Back—Not	39
Two at the Back	41
Alley…Oops	43
Key Shot Placements	45
Doing the Dink	47

Lob More Often	49
More on the Lob	52
Playing Against Lob-Happy Opponents	54
Overheads	56
Australian Formation	58
Playing Against the Australian Formation	59
The I Formation	61
Playing Against the I Formation	63
Always Defer the Serve	64
Get Your First Serve In	65
Serve Down the Middle	67
Keep Your Serving Options Open	69
The First Volley	71
Get the Return Back	74
When Your Partner Is Serving	76
When Your Partner Is Returning	79
Fixing a Losing Game	81
The Set-Up Volley	83
Ten Quick Tips	85

Introduction

You want to amp up your doubles game. Maybe you want to win your Saturday morning match more than once a month, or you're slipping down the pecking order on your league team.

What do you do?

If you're like most recreational players, you double down on improving your strokes. You sign up for lessons, serve buckets of balls, and drill your backhand. While all of these steps are good and will help your game, you won't see the results you're looking for as quickly as you would like.

Doubles is much more than the sum of your strokes. While you want to have some combination of a steady serve, consistent return, decent volley, reliable lob, dependable overhead, and good groundstrokes, you also have the twin challenges of playing with a partner and facing two opponents on the other side of the net.

The better—and faster—way to start winning more is to improve your match strategy. Rather than focusing on to hit the ball, concentrate on the where, when, and why you're hitting it.

Strategy is so important in doubles because you are playing as a team. All of us have been in those situations where your partner and you are each individually better than either of your opponents, but they beat you every time because they play together. They move as one, cutting off your angles. They always seem to be at the net, keeping you on the defensive. And they appear to know where you are going to hit the ball, waiting there to put it away.

You can be one of those players.

While there are numerous doubles strategies, the most effective for recreational players is to avoid unforced errors. In recreational doubles, eight out of every ten points are decided by unforced errors. Entire games can roll by without any of the players hitting a winner.

The primary cause of unforced errors is trying to do too much with the ball. You hit your first serve too hard and it plows straight into the net. You drive your return down the line and it lands wide. You smash your overhead and it hits the back fence on the fly.

When you play strategically, you don't have to try that hard. On every point, depending on where the four players are on the court, there are a limited number of correct shots to hit—often only one—and a correct position to take following your shot.

Here's an example. You're receiving serve in the ad court. The server has spun the serve wide to your backhand, pulling you outside the doubles sideline. You may have the urge to drive the ball down the line, but that would be a high-risk shot even if there weren't an opponent standing at the net. You might try a sharply angled cross-court sliced return, but from that depth, you will be hard pressed to keep the ball in the court. And, if you do, the server will likely be
well-positioned to hit a volley into the court that you've vacated.

The right shot—really the only one—is to lift a lob over the net player's head. You remove her from the equation and force her—and maybe the server—to retreat from the net. With one shot, you steal the serving team's advantage and give your team the opportunity to take the offensive.

On the following pages, you will learn how to adapt the concepts of strategic tennis to every situation you face on the doubles court.

We will also look at the importance of playing with the right partner, the need for constant and constructive communication between partners, and how developing a shared strategy can give your team an almost unassailable advantage in most recreational doubles matches.

Improving your tennis strokes significantly can take months or even years. Improving your tennis strategy enough to start winning the matches you're now losing takes only a few weeks. Knowing where to hit the ball and where to move will have a bigger impact on your game than adding a few miles per hour to your serve or working on your drop volley.

Basic Skills Needed for Strategic Recreational Doubles

Playing strategic doubles will take your game to the next level, but in order to make the most of the concepts in this book, you need to be able to hit five basic shots.

(Players with an NTRP rating above 3.0 may want to skip this chapter, although there's some good stuff here.)

Place your serve. You don't need to have a powerful first serve; rather you need to have high first-serve percentage. Aim for 70 percent or better. To achieve that—while not hitting powder-puff serves that have your opponents salivating—hit your serves with spin and depth and target the returner's backhand. If you and your partner want to execute planned poaches, you have to be able to place your serve down the middle.

Slice your backhand. You don't need to be able to hit winners with your backhand, but you must be able to keep the ball in play, because the first thing most opponents will do is attack your backhand. The sliced backhand is a great stroke in recreational doubles. It is so flexible, allowing you to drive, dink and lob. You can use it to hit from the baseline, to approach the net, to hit an angled volley, and, if you've been pulled wide or pushed deep, to lob.

Block your volley. It's great to be able to hit a winning volley, but it's not a necessity. Over the course of the point, game, set, and match, if you can consistently put your volleys back into the court, you will come out the winner. A simple volley, just blocking the ball back into the court, can be enough.

Spin your overhead. Hitting a smash feels oh-so good, but trying to put away every overhead puts a lot of pressure on your game and leads to unforced errors. You're better off spinning a medium-speed overhead at a short angle. Not only is it a safer shot, but you can pull apart your opponents' formation and get them scrambling.

Air out your lob. When you're opponents are camped out at the net, rather than trying to drive the ball past them, hit it over their heads. The lob has a fair claim to being the most important shot in recreational doubles. There is no better shot for getting you out of trouble. It keeps you in the point, gives you time to get in position, and forces your opponents to hit another shot.

No Unforced Errors

Doubles is a game of errors. Even at the highest levels of the game, two out of every three points end due to an error. In the recreational game, around eight out of ten points are decided by a mistake.

Given this reality, your best play in doubles is often to give your opponents the opportunity to make a mistake. Keeping the ball in play dramatically tilts the odds of winning the match in your favor.

Of course, you can't just push back every ball. You will lose quickly and both you and your partner will have a few ball-shaped bruises.

Here are several adaptations to limit your unforced errors.

Dial down the power. The leading cause of errors at the recreational level is trying to hit the ball too hard. When you try to blast the ball past your opponents, you hit more errors than winners. A small decrease in power will markedly improve your consistency. **Target the center of the court.** This is your safest shot and many recreational doubles teams focus on protecting their sidelines, leaving the middle open.

Take the net out of play. High-level doubles players hit the ball flat and low, because their opponents are so skilled at the net. As a result, they hit errors into the net three times more often than they hit long. You're not facing such adept volleyers, so take the net out of play as much as possible. (You have no chance of winning the point if your shot doesn't get over the net.) Add topspin to your shots to consistently clear the net.

Make the alleys your margin of error. While you want to take advantage of the increased width of the doubles court, land your shots inside the singles sidelines.

Make time. Doubles is fast-paced, with quick exchanges across the net. Stay on your toes and react instantly to your opponents' shots. Having more time to set up your shot immensely improves your consistency.

Move forward at every opportunity. If both you and your partner are at the net, you have a huge advantage. Not only are volleys far easier to hit consistently than ground strokes, but in their attempts to hit the ball past you, your opponents are more likely to make an error—or to give you an opening to put the ball away.

When you don't have a good shot, lob. The lob gives you the chance to turn a defensive situation into a neutral one. Not only do you keep the ball in play and give your team the opportunity to reset your formation, but—if you hit it high and deep enough—you push your opponents away from the net.

Stay patient. Keep the ball in play and use smart placements to give your opponents the opportunity to miss.

Communicate, Communicate, Communicate

Constant communication is a key component in any successful doubles team. Individually, you and your partner may be excellent strategists and players, but if you're not constantly communicating your intent to each other, you're not a team and have little hope of consistently winning matches.

Consider this situation: You're serving to the ad court. The receiver, like most recreational tennis players, has a stronger forehand than backhand, so you decide to serve wide to take advantage of that weakness. Your partner, on the other hand, knows that the best doubles serve to the ad court is down the T, so she cheats toward the middle. Both strategies are sound, but if you serve wide while your partner moves to the center, you've opened up almost half the court for the receiver to hit a winner.

Communication starts prior to the match, going over your strategy. If you play together often, it will probably be a short discussion.

Cover basic situations. Which of you is better for which side of the court? What do you want to do on first and second serves? Where do you prefer to serve in the ad and deuce courts? Who will cover which lobs? What hand signals—if any—will you use? Having agreed on these items from the start, your team will be focused and prepared from the first point.

If one or both of you has already played your opponents, take the time to talk about their strengths and weaknesses.

Keep your lines of communication open during the match.

When your team is serving, agree before each point where the serve is going and whether the poach is on. If for any reason you need to change the plan before the point starts, agree on the change. Banish as much uncertainty as possible before the point starts.

When you're receiving, discuss any tendencies you might have noticed in the server's placement or the net player's poaching. If you have nothing tactical to discuss, still get together just to give each other some encouragement.

During the point, call out directions when appropriate. On a ball hit between you and your partner, call "Mine" if you're going to take it. If you believe your partner has a better shot, call out "Yours" early and loudly.

If you think the ball is flying long or wide, call "Out" or "Bounce it." Occasionally you will be wrong and it will drop in. Don't get upset. Recreational tennis players tend to hit a lot of balls that would have landed out.

Trust your partner. Like you, she is trying as hard as she can. She didn't intentionally miss that easy put-away. If she is having a rough patch or even a rough match, encourage her. Let her know that you're confident that she's just about to get back in the groove.

Banish negativity because it doesn't help either of you. Even if you're down a set and two breaks, stay positive. After all, what's the alternative?

Keep criticism—even the "constructive" kind—to a minimum. Limit your suggestions to tactics. In other words, don't try to fix her backhand in the fourth game of the second set; instead, suggest that she serve down the middle because that will keep the ball in the center of the court (where she can play her forehand).

After the match, take a couple of minutes to discuss how the match went—both individually and as a team. Even if you may not play together again, this debriefing will give you insights into what you can work on and try to do better next time. Recently, in one of these post-match meetings, my partner pointed out that I went to the well too many times with my favorite shot—a tightly angled soft volley. While it caught out our opponents several times in the early games, later on they were ready for it and had several easy put-aways—including on match point. Lesson learned.

Keep Moving Forward

Play as if the court is sloped downward from the baseline to the net.

The hallmark of all good doubles players—and teams—is that they're always looking for the opportunity to move forward and take control of the net.

On your serve, look to come in behind both your first AND second serves. Your first volley is essentially an approach shot to get you to the net.

When returning serve, set up as far forward as you can while consistently keeping the ball in play. If you have the opportunity—the serve lands short or the server stays back—follow your return into the net.

In doubles, there is no such thing as settling into a baseline rally. At times you may be pushed back by your opponent's lob and trapped there by their overheads, but always be calculating how both you and your partner can move forward again.

Protect the Middle of the Court

Recreational doubles players tend to play too wide. In a misguided effort to protect the alleys or to try to cover the entire court, we fail to protect the center, even though that's where most shots in doubles go.

When you're playing the net, lean towards the middle. More than eight out of ten service returns are hit cross-court, so when your partner is serving, be ready to poach on anything hit too close to the center strap.

During the point, your opponents' best shot is to keep the ball in the middle of the court. The net is lower so they have a larger margin for error. By protecting the middle, you put yourself in the best position to reply to their most likely shots, or you may induce them to try to hit the ball down the line, which is a difficult shot and leads to unforced errors.

When you're serving, hit your serve down the middle and approach closer to the center line. Your service placement will keep most returns in the middle of the court, giving you the opportunity to hit your first volley—or your partner to poach. If your opponents try to hit where you aren't, they will need to hit high-risk shots that bring the sidelines into play.

Play the Percentages

Winning in doubles is about playing the percentages. If you and your partner are hitting high percentage shots and/or your opponents are hitting low percentage shots, you are going to win most of the time.

High percentage shots balance two key characteristics. First—and most importantly—they are shots that you are confident that you can keep in play. Second, they are shots that put pressure on your opponents. Hitting a shoulder-high floater down the middle of the court is not a high-percentage shot, because while you can hit it consistently, your opponents can put it away for a winner just as consistently.

Playing the percentages starts with the first serve. Rather than smacking a serve that has a 50-50 chance (or less) of landing in, spin a three-quarter-speed serve down the middle of the court. Your opponent will have a play on the ball, but you and your partner will be well positioned to deal with any return.

When returning serve, rather than trying to hit a winner, hit cross-court with either underspin or topspin.

Whenever the speed, spin, or height of your opponent's shot is too much for you to handle, hit a defensive lob. When you lob your goal is not to hit a winner, rather it is to get the ball over the head of the net player(s).

Recreational players go for difficult shots because they want to end the point too soon. Concentrate on keeping the ball in play and let your opponents give in to the temptation of going for a high-risk shot.

Wait for the high ball that you can put away.

Don't worry about being predictable. There are only so many high-percentage shots in any given situation and your opponents will eventually figure out which ones you prefer to hit. That's okay. You're always better off hitting the right shot than going for a more difficult, lower percentage shot.

Hit, for example, the vast majority of your service returns cross-court with as tight an angle as you can conjure without flirting with the sideline. Your opponents know you are going to hit there, but unless they change their formation or overcommit to stopping you, it's your best shot. And if they shift their formation to stop the cross-court return, hitting down-the-line suddenly becomes high-percentage.

Control—Not Power

We've all been there, looking across the net at two grizzled doubles veterans. Maybe they're both a generation older, maybe one has a huge knee brace, and maybe the other is overweight. And then the match starts and they proceed to slice and dice their way to an easy win, hitting every shot where you aren't and never giving you a free point.

Hitting with power is not the key to winning recreational doubles matches. It's more likely the reason for losing them.

Doubles is about control. Keeping the ball in play. Keeping your opponents moving. Keeping them guessing. Keeping them from setting up to hit a clean shot.

And then, when you have opened up their court, hitting an easy put-away.

With two opponents on the other side of the net, you gain little advantage by hitting the ball as hard as you can. In most instances, they will be well positioned to return your killer drives, and you are more likely to make an unforced error.

Take, for example, the overhead. If your opponents hit a mid-court or deep lob and have time to set up behind their baseline, they have a high probability of lobbing back your smash. If you keep trying to hit overheads past them, you're keeping them in the point and increasing the odds that you will smack the ball long or into the net. Instead, spin your overhead wide, aiming for the T where the service line meets the singles sideline. While one of your opponents will likely reach the ball, she will have to hit a much more difficult shot.

Serves are another good example. Doubles players who bash their first serves tend to have low first serve percentages, putting all of the pressure on their second serve. By hitting your first serve to force the return you want from your opponent, you will have a higher first-serve percentage and win more of your service games.

Control also gives you the opportunity to exploit any weaknesses that you uncover in your opponents. If one—or both—of them is slow or has a weak overhead or can't hit a backhand volley, you can take advantage.

Doubles Is Won at the Net

Doubles matches are won at the net. Even if you and your partner don't volley well, you will still win most of your matches if you play a lot of points from the net.

Based on match statistics—excluding the serve and the return of serve because they must be played from the baseline—80 percent of points are won by the players at the net.

The advantages of being at the net are numerous. The volley is easier to hit than the passing shot and you have a wider range of angles. Your opponent's time to hit her passing shot is shortened and her options are limited. That's not to say that the volley is easy.

The challenge of the volley is time. Because the ball is only traveling half the length of the court, you have half the time to react, set up, and hit the ball—about two-tenths of a second.

Further complicating the stroke is that the majority of volleys are hit on the backhand side, which tends to be weaker. The backhand is more common because opponents target that side and human physiology dictates that you can only hit a forehand volley when the ball is outside your right hip (if you're right-handed). All other volleys—including those hit straight at you—are hit with your backhand.

Fortunately you can win at recreational doubles with only a basic block volley that you can direct to one side of the court or the other. There's no backswing. It can be as simple as sticking your racquet face in the flight of the ball. If you can put a little underspin on it, that's great, but not necessary.

Blocked volleys don't tend to be put-away shots so you will probably have to hit more than one volley during the point, but because of the overwhelming advantage that you and your partner have at the net, you'll still win most of the time.

Here are several keys to improving your success at the net.

One-two punch. The essential doubles volleying strategy is to hit an angled volley to pull your opponents wide and then volley down the middle; or to volley down the middle to draw your opponents to the center of the court and then to hit an angled volley for a winner

Crowd the net. The closer that you get to the net, the more you take it out of play. A chunked volley that would tumble into the bottom of the net if you were in the middle of your service box will drop over for a winner when you are on top of the net. Setting up close to the net also shrinks the angles for your opponent's passing shots. One danger of being too aggressive is you open yourself up to the lob, so you need to be ready to backtrack.

Volley Deep. Match statistics show that the deep volley accounts for about one-third of all winning points in doubles. It's a difficult shot for your opponents to return because it comes at them so fast and often at an angle. Deep, however, doesn't mean aiming for the baseline; target your shot to land just past the service line. The deep volley is even more potent if you set it up with a short angled volley.

Attack the High Ball. Never let a volley drop. Whenever you see a high ball, move in swiftly so you can hit down on it. Once the ball is below the top of the net, you have to hit up, which gives the advantage to your opponents.

Target the Middle. When you have a difficult volley, hit the ball down the middle. It's the safest shot and limits your opponents' angles, so even if they hit the ball back, you remain in control at the net.

Importance of Court Positioning

Good court positioning can "force" unforced errors.

When you move in to cut off your opponents' angles and limit their options, you will win a lot of points without even having to hit the next shot because they will hit high-risk shots to get the ball past you.

You and your partner have complete control over your court position. Whether it's before the ball has been served or in the middle of the point, strategic doubles partners constantly move in their court to put their opponents at a disadvantage.

In reality, you and your partner cannot cover the entire court, but often you can limit your opponents' ability to hit the best shot at that moment or their favorite shot. If, for instance, an opponent has a great cross-court return, shift into the Australian formation or the I formation to take that away from her.

During the point, pinch toward the center of the court. Most shots in doubles go over the low part of the net; make sure you and your partner have those shots covered. And agree beforehand which of you will take the balls hit down the middle. Few things in doubles are more frustrating than forcing your opponent to hit down the center and then watching the ball pass between the two of you.

If you are crosscourt from the opponent who is about to hit the ball, use the net strap to guide your positioning. Always keep a straight line between her, the net strap and you. If she is hitting from her alley, for example, move over into your alley. If she is closer to the center of the court, then slide that way. This keeps you in the middle of her angle of reply, which is the full range of possible shots that she can hit.

If you are the net player on the same side of the court as the opponent hitting the ball, mirror her. As your opponent moves, slide with her, moving closer to the sideline or to the center as she does. Because the two of you are on the same side of the court, she won't be able to generate sufficient angles to get the ball past you.

Importance of Court Positioning at the Net

When you and your partner are at the net, you have an overwhelming advantage, but not even the doubles team of Sam Querrey (6'6") and John Isner (6'10") can cover the entire net all of the time. To prevent your opponents from hitting into the seams between you—and over your heads—you need to move strategically.

Shade toward the center of the court because most shots in a doubles point are hit there.

Slide your formation along the net to force your opponents to hit shots they don't want to hit. If your partner moves wide to strike the ball, for example, shift to cover the middle of the court. Your opponents have the choice of trying to thread the needle down the line or acutely cross-court, hitting right at one of you, or…lobbing.

When you've pushed your opponents into a situation where their only option is to lob, both you and your partner need to be ready to backtrack.

At any time, if you have chance to cut across in front of your partner to put away the ball, go for it.

If all four players are at the net, move closer and crowd the center to pressure your opponents to come up with a great volley.

Poaching

Successful doubles teams poach. The poach is one of the most powerful weapons in the doubles arsenal. Even if neither your partner nor you has a great volley—or even a particularly good one—you can still expect to win two out of every three points when you poach.

Here are nine keys to strategic poaching:

Vary your set-up position. Give your opponents something to think about before your partner serves by changing where you set up. On one point, start closer to the center line. On the next, take a couple of steps toward the sideline. Once your partner starts her service motion, move to your intended position—or poach.

Honor your commitment. If you tell your partner before she serves that you're going to poach, you must follow through. Even if your opponent hits a weak return behind you, keep going because your partner is already moving to cover the space you vacated. If you stop to hit the volley, you leave half of the court undefended.

Move. You don't actually need to poach a lot to be effective. Merely moving around like you're going to poach can be enough to distract your opponent. The rules of tennis state that you must not intentionally distract your opponents, so don't go overboard.

Fake the poach. This takes moving to the next level. Faking the poach, by taking one or two steps toward the center line—or even by just shifting your weight in that direction—can cause your opponent to try to change her shot direction. Maybe she'll stick with her cross-court, but she'll go for a wider, higher-risk shot. Or she may try to hit behind you, in which case you will have remained in the ideal spot to put the ball away.

Track the opponent's movement. When you're looking to poach on your partner's serve or on any subsequent shots, watch your opponent. If she moves wide to hit the ball, you're better off staying put, because she has more shot options and more time to hit the ball. If she moves to hit the ball closer to the center, look to poach because her options and angles are limited.

Volley to the Ts. Limit yourself to two target areas when you poach. If you meet the ball near the center of the court, aim for the service line T down the middle. If you have moved farther across the court to hit the ball, target the T where the service line meets the singles sideline. Always hit in the direction in which you're moving and continue moving in that direction. One of the immutable rules of doubles is to never hit back in the direction from which you came.

Put the ball away. When you poach, you need to hit a winner. Unless it's planned—in which case, your partner is moving to cover the court you're vacating—poaching leaves big holes in your formation. Of course, you're not going to hit a winner every time, but a poacher aims to win about two out of three poach attempts.

Adapt. As the match progresses, you may need to alter your poaching strategy. If, for example, the service returner is whipping low, wide, dipping shots that you have to strain just to get back, don't continue to poach. Instead, protect your side of the court and count on your partner to get the ball back; or switch to the I formation or Australian formation. If she keeps lobbing over your head, step back a pace or two to take away that shot. And if she's got a particularly potent down-the-line drive, shade that way to force her to return cross-court. On the other hand, if she floats her returns, poach more often.

Just Say No. In the run of play, you start to poach and then realize that you won't be able to hit a penetrating shot. What do you do? Let the ball go through to your partner. Your team is actually better off if you stop and slide back into position, because when you poach you unbalance your team's formation and leave large swathes of the court undefended. (This doesn't apply to the planned poach on your partner's serve; in that instance, if you signal a poach, you must go through with it.)

Returning Serve

Returning serve in doubles is about beating the odds. Everything favors the serving team. They get to start the point. They even get a second try if they miss the first one. Both of them know where the serve is going. And the server is well on her way to joining her partner at the net by the time you hit your return.

According to match statistics, the serving team wins 70 percent of all service points. Even when you get the serve back in play, the serving team still wins about six out of ten points.

How do you beat the odds?

Get your return in play.

Nothing good can happen unless you're in the point, so your most important task is to put the ball in play. Don't give away any free points.

Returners miss their returns because they try to hit the ball too hard, too flat, and/or too angled. Again, match statistics tell the story. Returners hit winners on only 12 percent of their shots time and hit errors on 20 percent. By not going for elusive winners and by focusing on eliminating errors, you shift the odds a little more in your favor.

The serving team retains the advantage, however, because they're taking control of the net. They haven't quite done it yet, though, and that's the chink in their armor. Your best strategy is to direct all—or almost all—of your returns at the onrushing server, and—within your primary directive of keeping the ball in play—to make her first volley as difficult as possible.

Most servers will target your backhand. A good return is to slice or chop, a short, underspin shot hit wide and short. The shot has four advantages. It is safe, which means you will get more returns into play. The slow pace and low bounce make it difficult for the server to put much sting in her first volley. That slow pace also gives you the opportunity to move forward on your return. And its wide trajectory makes it difficult for the net player to poach.

Most recreational players haven't developed a reliable forehand slice, so your best shot when the serve is hit to your forehand is the topspin drive. Again it's a relatively safe shot and its spin can cause problems for the server on the volley. The topspin allows you to hit the shot wide, increasing the difficulty of any poach. Because of the shot's pace, however, you likely won't be able to come in behind your return.

Decide where you are going to aim your return before your opponent begins her service motion. Once you've decided on your shot placement, ignore the movement of the server and the net player and concentrate solely on the ball. It's too difficult for most recreational players to base their shot placement on the movements of the other team.

Hit almost all of your returns cross-court and as wide as you can hit consistently. The only reason to aim an occasional return down the line is to take advantage of an overzealous net player who too early betrays her intention to poach.

One of the best—but least utilized—service returns is to lob over the head of the net player. This shot is especially effective against an active net player, but you can hit it at any time. Not only do you eliminate the poach, but you blunt the serving team's strategic advantages. Either the net player has to move back or the server has to break off her approach to chase down the lob. One word of caution: your lob must clear the net player or you're giving away an easy overhead smash.

When facing a second serve, look for every opportunity to come in behind your return. Prior to the serve, move in a couple of steps and then step into your shot. If the server doesn't follow her serve or you hit a penetrating return, move forward.

Choosing Teams

In recreational doubles, you typically play two types of matches: Saturday morning matches with your friends and league/tournament matches. Your approach to choosing a partner varies significantly between these two instances.

For your Saturday morning doubles, your choice of partner is limited. In most cases, you're choosing from just three other players, and the decision-making process comes with lots of baggage. Who played with whom last week? Who just can't play with whom? What combinations make the teams most even? These factors tend to outweigh the more strategic consideration of assembling the best team.

When you're playing in leagues or tournaments, strategic concerns are paramount. According to one doubles analyst, "teamwork" accounts for about 25 percent of a doubles team's success.

The most important factor in successful doubles teams is mutual respect. You need to like your partner and she needs to like you. Tennis is a game of unforced errors and they will quickly undermine a team that doesn't have a strong foundation. You won't win and you won't have fun, so what's the point.

Most tennis strategists suggest that the best doubles teams feature players with complementary strengths—one steady player and one aggressive player. The steady partner plays the strategic game and works the ball to set up her partner. The aggressive player has carte blanche to go for risky shots and clean winners.

That strategy may work in the upper echelons of the game, but recreational doubles teams tend to work better when the partners have similar strengths. Next time you're at a tournament, check out the winning teams. Most often, you'll find they are players who are mirror images of each other.

Two like-thinking players are better able to execute their strategy on the court. While two complementary recreational players can develop a strategy that highlights each other's individual strengths, that adds an extra layer of complexity that most of us have neither the skill nor practice time to master. Doubles is tough enough; keep your strategy simple.

Different mindsets can also cause rifts between the partners. An aggressive player who makes a lot of errors can grate on a steady player. At the same time, a steady player who fails to go for a putaway can annoy a net rusher. Two players who approach the game the same will understand what each is trying to do and be better able to support each other.

Even when both of you have the same mindset, each of you will be better at certain strokes. As best you can, find a partner whose game complements your own. If, for example, your overhead isn't particularly good, look for a partner who has a strong one. If your backhand is weaker, find a player with a better one.

Which Side of the Court?

One of the first decisions you will have to make as a doubles team is which side of the court each of you will take.

Conventional wisdom suggests that the stronger player takes the ad court, because many critical points start there, i.e. 40-30, 30-40, and all ad points.

This reasoning, however, doesn't hold up. More points are actually played from the deuce side—after all, every game starts with a serve to that side—and it has its fair share of critical points, i.e. 40-15, 15-40, and all deuce points.

Here's a simple two-step process to decide who plays which side of the court.

First, analyze your and your partner's relative strengths and weaknesses.

Who handles pressure better? She should play the ad court.

Who is more aggressive? This one can go either way, but on balance, the more aggressive player should take the deuce court because if she hits a winner—or a penetrating shot that turns into a winner—you're at ad point; if, however, her aggression produces an unforced error, you're still in the game.

Better cross-court forehand? Deuce court.

Better cross-court backhand? Ad court.

The partner with the better overhead takes the ad court (if both of you are right-handed), because the ad-court player returns lobs hit down the center,

Better forehand volley? Ad court.

Better backhand volley? Deuce court

You get the idea. Based on this analysis, you can determine who is better suited to take which side.

The second step is to do the opposite. Between sets or matches, switch sides.

After a few matches you'll figure out which alignment works best for your team. It may be the opposite of what your initial analysis suggested, because team synergy is often more important than the individual strengths and weaknesses of the partners.

Whose Shot Is It?

During the point, your opponents hit a shot down the middle. Whose ball is it?

Here's a simple guide.

On every middle ball, with the exception of the lob, the player closer to the net has dibs. She decides in that first instant if she can make an effective play on the ball. If she can, it's hers; if you can't, she leaves the ball for her partner. The deeper player, then, has to be prepared to hit every ball coming down the middle.

If both partners are at the same court depth, whoever can hit a forehand takes the shot. If both have forehands to the middle (right- and left-handed partners), the stronger player hits the ball.

In a quick-fire exchange at the net, the player who hit the previous shot takes the next one.

An angled cross-court ball hit between partners at the net is taken by the cross-court player.

On lobs, the deeper player is responsible. If both players are at the net, the cross-court player retrieves the lob. She also tells her partner what she wants her to do: stay at the net, slide to the other side of the court, or retreat to the baseline.

All things being equal, the partner with the stronger overhead plays from the ad court (if both are right-handed), because that player takes all lobs hit down the middle.

It bears repeating that on shots down the middle, unless it's blindingly obvious which player will hit the ball, prepare to hit every shot.

Mixed Doubles Problem

The biggest impediment to the success of most mixed doubles teams is the male ego.

To the men, I say: Get over yourself.

When you step on the tennis court, there are no gender roles. You are two partners looking to win matches and have a good time doing it. So, if your partner is better at some—or all—aspects of the game, take advantage of that for the good of your team.

If she has a better serve, she should serve first.

If she has a better cross-court backhand return, she should take the ad court.

If her overhead is better, she should take most of the lobs.

If she's got a better strategic or tactical sense for the game, she should take the lead.

And to the women, I say: Assert yourself

Don't let the male ego undermine your chances to win matches—and to have fun.

Winning the Key Points

Matches are won and lost on a few key points. Play those points better than your opponents and your winning percentage will soar.

Tennis books (including this one) tell you to focus on every point regardless of the score. Although that's a worthwhile goal, it isn't going to happen. Your attention is going to wax and wane, and so will your opponents'. Accept that reality and concentrate on winning the points in the match that are truly decisive.

What are the key points? Obviously break points (regardless of whether you are serving or returning), game points, set points, and match points are decisive, but are there others?

In his book *Winning Ugly*, Brad Gilbert asserts that several other points in a game are critical. He calls these the setup points, because they set up a game point. They are 30-15, 15-30, 30-love, love-30, 30-30, and deuce. He asserts that if you get more ad-point opportunities—or prevent your opponent from getting them—you will probably win the match.

Gilbert's insight can have a profound impact on your game. If you and your partner turn up your focus on the setup points, which your opponents probably consider run of the mill, you have a hidden advantage.

Plan with your partner prior to the match how you will play the decisive points. Determining your strategy up front increases your chances of winning these points because you'll know what you want to do.

Emphasize your strengths. Don't lose these points; force your opponent to win them.

Stay in the moment. The points last only a few shots. You can focus your concentration for that long.

Most recreational players subconsciously try to end decisive points too quickly, going for the big serve or the winner on the return. Instead, be patient. Keep the ball in play and let your opponents give in to that temptation.

Two Captains

A doubles team has a strategic captain and a tactical captain…and they're not always the same person.

The strategic captain is the better player. One of you is always the better doubles player. Maybe she doesn't actually have better strokes, but the teams she's on just seem to win. Before and after you play—and between points—this player keeps the team focused on your strategy, making tweaks to the plan as the match unfolds, and highlighting your opponents' weaknesses for you to exploit.

The tactical captain changes depending on the flow of the point. At the beginning of the point, the server or the service returner takes command, because she is behind the net player and can see the whole court. She is in a better position to call out directions, such as whether to let a ball go, whose ball it is, and whether to cover the lob, come back, or switch sides of the court.

If in the course of play the two partners switch positions, they switch roles as well.

The net player also has leadership responsibilities, calling out directions if play demands, such as recognizing that the opponents are about to hit a lob or calling a switch because she's poaching.

One-Up, One-Back—Not

The most common formation in recreational tennis is also the least effective—the one-up and one-back configuration.

It's easy to see why recreational doubles teams use this formation. Not only is it how we typically start the point, but it feels right. We have one player to cover the net and one player to cover the back.

On top of that, hitting that first volley coming in behind your serve is one of the hardest shots in the game: You're moving forward; you're stuck in no-man's land between the baseline and the net; and an opponent is perched just across the net. The urge to stay back and hit from the baseline is powerful.

Fight that urge. In almost every instance, the one-up and one-back formation puts your team at a disadvantage.

The fundamental weakness of the formation is court coverage. With one-up and one-back, you leave wide swathes of the court unprotected. The most obvious hole in your defense is a cross-court shot hit into the space behind the net player. It's an easy and safe shot for your opponents to hit and there's little your partner and you can do against it. The second hole is the tight volley in front of the baseline player. Again it's a relatively easy shot for your opponents and almost impossible for you or your partner to reach.

That's not to say that you should rush forward on every serve regardless of the game circumstances or your particular volleying skills. After all, a lot of recreational players have trouble with serving and volleying. So, if you lose more points than you win when you come in after your serve, it makes no sense to keep doing it.

In these situations—or any other where you don't feel comfortable coming in behind your serve—pull the net player back so you have two at the back.

And if your opponents hit a short ball, you and your partner can move forward as a team and take the net.

Two at the Back

The second best formation in recreational doubles is both players at the baseline. That's not to say it's a good formation—the only truly "good" formation is when both of you are at the net—but it is far better than having one partner up and one partner back.

The two-back formation is defensive. You want to employ it in situations when your opponents have an advantage and you and your partner need to hunker down.

The three most common situations for two at the back are when the returners are punishing your serve, when they have a punishing serve, and when a lob gets behind you.

If an opponent has a potent return of serve—or you don't have a penetrating serve—pull the net player back towards the baseline. You cede the net to your opponents, but you will be in the point.

When receiving, if the on-rushing server is hitting winners off your returns, bring the net player back to the baseline to take the sting out of that first volley.

When a lob gets over your head and you need to retreat to the baseline to retrieve it, tell your partner to come back. Your best response is to hit a defensive lob, and you don't want to leave her stranded at the net when your opponents are hitting overheads.

In anticipation of those overheads, position yourselves behind the baseline, shading slightly to the center of the court. Expect to have to hit another lob and another…and another. Take heart: It's actually easier to keep hitting defensive lobs than to keep smacking overheads.

The most important characteristic of the two-back formation is that it is transitional. As soon as the flow of the point allows, you and your partner want to move forward and take the net.

If you get a short ball, step in and hit a drive up the middle. Recreational doubles players tend to stand too far apart, so targeting the middle of the court is not only a safe shot, but it can be effective.

If one of your lobs drops behind your opponents, you and your partner can move forward to the service line. Your opponents' best reply to your lob is to put up their own lob, so you will be in a good position to hit an overhead. If they're foolish enough to drive the ball, step forward and hit an angled volley winner.

Alley…Oops

Doubles matches aren't won in the alleys, but they can be lost there.

The alley can be enticing—six additional feet on either side of the court into which to hit a blistering winner—but in the recreational game, your best strategy is to look upon the alley as less of a target and more as a margin of error.

The foundation of strategic doubles is keeping the ball in play. You want to avoid playing high-risk shots, and balls aimed into the alley are definitely high risk. In the heat of the point, they require too fine an edge.

Instead, make the singles sideline your target. In most instances the angle will still be wide enough to be a winner or to pull your opponent far off the court.

On your side of the net, don't get hung up on defending the alley. Certainly be aware that it is part of the court and position yourself to cover as much of the court as possible, but most shots are hit cross court or down the middle. Being in a good position to reply to those shots is much more important.

And just as the alley can entice you into unforced errors, it can do the same for your opponents. If you give them a sliver of opportunity to hit down the line, they will miss more than they will make. If you are really lucky, they will hit a beautiful winner into the alley early in the match. Smile as you congratulate them, because you can be confident that they will spend the rest of the match trying—and mostly failing—to replicate that moment of glory.

Key Shot Placements

Where to hit the ball in doubles can be boiled down to two simple instructions:

Hit deep-to-deep

Hit short-to-short*

When you are deeper in the court, hit the ball towards the deeper opponent. On the service return, this means you are hitting back to the server. If she comes in behind her serve, be ready to reply to her first volley. If she stays back, look to come in behind your return.

If you are at the baseline and both opponents are at the net, your best deep-to-deep shot is the lob.

One of the biggest mistakes in recreational doubles is hitting deep-to-short. It doesn't work in any instance. If you are deep and your partner is close to the net, you put her in harm's way of a hard-struck volley. If you are both at the baseline, you open up your court to a sharp-angled volley.

When you are close to the net, aim short. If the ball is above the level of the net and you can hit down on it, aim at the net player's feet or at the Ts (either the center T or where the service line meets the singles sideline.) The pace and the placement will make it difficult for your opponent to generate a penetrating return.

*The one instance when you may have to hit short to deep is when you are in the forecourt and the ball is below the level of the net. You can't put any heat on the ball, so hitting it at the opposing net player invites trouble. If both of your opponents are at the net, aim your shot deep a down the middle.

Doing the Dink

The urge to rip a passing shot through two opponents poised at the net is almost primal, but it is also a low-percentage shot. They are well positioned to reach almost any driven ball and the pace and height of your passing shot make it easy to volley away.

If you're at the baseline, your best—only?—option is the lob. From the mid-court forward, do the dink.

The dink is a soft, tightly angled, underspin shot that lands well inside the cross-court service box. It is difficult for your opponents to return because of its tight angle and dipping trajectory. Unless they are right on top of the net, the ball will drop below the net cord before they can reach it. They will have to hit up on the ball, so they won't be able to put too much power behind it.

For most recreational players, the dink works better on the backhand side, because while most of us have a serviceable backhand slice, not many of us can chip the forehand with any consistency. If you can slice your forehand or want to work to develop that shot, go for it.

The dink is really only effective when you are inside the service line, because you can hit the ball at enough of an angle to keep it inside the opposing service box.

Because of the slow pace of the shot, you don't want to dink from behind the baseline. In the time the ball takes to cross the net, your opponent will be able to move in, make a cup of coffee, eat a pastry, and then hit a put-away volley. (She won't have quite that much time, but you get the idea.)

Lob More Often

The lob is an underutilized shot in recreational doubles. That's a strategic mistake because it's one of the most effective weapons in your doubles arsenal.

Hitting a defensive lob pulls at least one—and probably both—of your opponents away from the net, giving your team the chance to move forward.

When your opponents have pulled you off the court or pushed you deep behind the baseline, the lob keeps you in the point. Lobs are also a lot easier to hit than overheads, so even though your smash-hitting opponents theoretically have the advantage, they still have to put away the ball with a shot that most recreational players have trouble hitting consistently.

And if you air out the ball frequently, you put the fear of the lob into your opponents. They will be on their back foot whenever they're at the net, always ready to retreat.

The most frequent lob in recreational doubles is the high defensive lob hit with underspin.* This shot has the height to clear the net player, stays in the court, and bounces almost vertically, forcing your opponent to generate all the power in her reply.

Lobs aren't meant to be winners. When you put the ball up, your goal is to get the point back on an even keel, to upset your opponents' strategic formation, and—depending on their reply—to give your team the opportunity to move forward.

Your lob needs enough height and depth to clear the net player. Otherwise it's less of a lob and more of a floating return that puts your partner in mortal danger.

The net player may backtrack to try to hit an overhead in the mid-court, but because her momentum is taking her away from the net, she won't be able to put too much oomph into the ball.

When lobbing on the service return, always hit over the opposing net player's head. (A cross-court lob puts the ball onto the racquet of the onrushing server.) Lobbing over the net player prevents your opponents from taking control of the net. Either the net player has to backtrack to retrieve the lob or the server has to move across the court rather than forward.

During the run of play, however, your best lob is cross-court. Angles make all the difference. Cross-court is the longest dimension of the court, giving you a bigger margin for error. Additionally, lobbing ad-court to ad-court usually puts the ball on the opponent's backhand side, which is a tough overhead to hit.

If your lob is deep enough to force your opponents back to their baseline, you and your partner can move forward to the service line. Don't rush the net, however, because the best response to your lob is another lob. At the service line, you are in an ideal position to hit most overheads. And, if your opponent attempts a passing shot, you are well positioned to move forward and volley.

If you and your partner are trapped behind the baseline, lobbing from deep while your opponents are camping out in the forecourt and smashing overheads, don't despair. All is not lost. Match statistics show that your opponents' advantage diminishes with each successive lob that you hit. Recreational players have much more difficulty hitting overhead after overhead than lob after lob. Keep putting the ball up high enough and deep enough and they'll likely make an error before you do.

*Unless it's a reliable weapon in your arsenal, the offensive lob is not a good shot in recreational doubles. It is difficult to hit well and frequently lands short, leaving your team open to the smash from the net.

More on the Lob

In doubles you want to keep the ball in front of you so you can move forward and take control of the net. When your opponents lob over your head, however, you have to recalibrate your attack.

If both you and your partner are at the net when your opponent hits a deep lob, both of you must retreat to the baseline. One of the more effective tactics is for the cross-court player to move diagonally to retrieve the lob and for the other player to cross diagonally to protect the other side of the court.

Always return a deep lob with a defensive lob. After hitting their lob, your opponents will most likely move forward to take the now vacated net. If you try to drive the ball, they can cut it off for an angled volley. A deep lob will keep them in their backcourt.

Hit your lob with the expectation that your opponents will be able to return it. If you try to hit a deep winner, you will too often hit the ball past the baseline. The role of the lob is to keep you in the point.

But…when you're hitting a backhand lob, make sure that you hit it deep enough. Recreational players tend to have a weak backhand lob and often hit too short a shot, which becomes an easy put-away for your opponents.

When your lob isn't deep enough and your opponents have an overhead, set up one or two feet behind the baseline. If you are cross-court from the opponent hitting the overhead, position yourself in a line with her and the net strap. If you are on the same side of the court as your overhead-hitting opponent, mirror her position on the court.

Always lean toward the center of the court because that's the prime target area for overheads.

Playing Against Lob-Happy Opponents

Every so often, you will play against opponents who hit lobs on almost every shot. They return your serve with a lob and then sit back at the baseline, hitting deep lob after deep lob. Because this is their primary shot, they've got it grooved and can keep hitting it all day long.

What do you do?

What you don't do is try to beat them at their own game. If you do, you've already lost because they've pulled you out of your winning strategy and into their's.

Instead, adapt your game to take advantage of the inherent weaknesses of the lobbing game.

Keep moving forward. Regardless of who you're playing, doubles is won at the net, so if they're willing to cede the net to you, take it. Don't, however, crowd the net. You don't need to because they are not going to try to drive the ball past you or hit a dink. Instead set up a pace or two deeper—maybe halfway between the service line and the net.

If they hit a shallow lob, close the net and angle a volley into the service box. It's a likely winner against most baseline-hugging lobbers.

If you're hitting an overhead from mid-court, take some pace off your shot and spin it towards the singles sideline. Your opponent will probably get to it and put up another lob, but you've unstitched their defensive formation.

Against other opponents, if a lob gets behind you, your partner and you typically need to retreat to the baseline and put up a defensive lob. That's not necessarily the case when playing lob-addicted opponents. Rather than come in behind their successful lobs, they often stay rooted to the baseline, so you are free to hit a groundstroke. Rather than hit a drive, however, which puts the ball in their lob wheelhouse, hit topspin or slice. It's harder to hit a good lob off a high bouncing ball or a low skidding one.

Stay patient. Their goal is to entice you to go for too good a shot, which too often results in an unforced error. Hit angled shots that make it more difficult for them to hit their lobs consistently and wait for balls that you can put away.

Overheads

You're going to get lobbed, so here's a strategic approach to overheads.

Everything else being equal, the player on your team with the better overhead should play the ad court (if both of you are right-handed) because that player takes all lobs hit down the center.

On high lobs, let the ball bounce before hitting your overhead. You gain nothing by taking the ball out of the air, because in most instances your opponents will have had time to set up defensively. Bouncing the ball gives you time to consider your options and makes your overhead a much higher percentage shot.

If you're hitting an overhead at the net, smash it away.

When you are deeper in the court, however, placement is more important than pace. Hit your overheads in the holes into your opponents' formation.

The net player takes the lob if she can reach it within two quick backtracking steps. If she can't, the ball belongs to the cross-court player.

The deeper partner is always responsible for setting the court coverage, telling her partner whether to retreat to the baseline, slide across to the other side of the court, or stay put.

From the mid-court, the most effective overhead is a cross-court shot that lands inside the service box.. The key to this shot is to hit it like a second serve. This shot works especially well if your opponents have set up at the baseline.

If the lob gets over your head, base your shot selection on where your opponents are. If they stayed at their own baseline, drive the ball deep and come forward again; if they came in behind their shot, lob them.

Australian Formation

If your opponents are beating you with their cross-court service returns, switch to the Australian Formation, in which the net player lines up on the same side of the court as the server.

The Australian Formation disrupts the return game of a lot of recreational players because it takes away the cross-court shot, which accounts for about 85 percent of service returns.

After hitting the serve, the server moves diagonally into the forecourt. Unless the returner drives a really good ball down the alley, the server can cover that side of the court. On second serves—or if she doesn't have a strong serve—the server moves parallel to the baseline to give herself more time to retrieve the return.

Always serve down the T when using the Australian Formation, because you cut down the returner's angles. If you serve wide, you open up too much of the court.

Use the Australian Formation as a change of pace. It can throw off a strong returner or upset the rhythm of the returning team. It usually doesn't work as a primary formation, however, because it leaves too much of the court undefended and competent opponents will start picking you apart.

Defending Against the Australian Formation

Every serving formation has a weakness and in the Australian Formation—in which the net player starts on the same side of the court as the server—it's defending against returns down the middle.

Opponents resort to the Australian Formation to counter your cross-court returns. By taking away that shot, they hope to disrupt your rhythm and formation.

When your opponents line up in the Australian Formation, adjust your team's positioning. The returner slides a pace or two closer to the center, because in the Australian Formation, almost every serve is directed down the T. The net player also moves closer to the center line because the cross-court return is not on.

Typically, recreational players facing the Australian formation will try to return serve down the line, figuring the server won't be able to cover the shot. That, however, is a low-percentage shot.

Your best return is to drive the ball down the center of the court. The net player typically doesn't poach in the Australian Formation because she moved over specifically to protect against the cross-court return, and the server is moving past the center to cover the open court. Shots down the middle will often split their formation.

Your second-best return is the cross-court lob. It's a relatively safe shot and you're hitting into the space that the server has just vacated.

Against second or weak serves, a good option is to dink down the line and approach. It can be a hard shot for the server to reach.

The I Formation

Serving from the I Formation can throw off opponents with a strong all-around return game.

In the I Formation, the net player straddles the center line and crouches low to allow for the serve to pass over her head. Prior to the serve, she signals behind her back in which direction she is going to move. The server covers the other side of the court.

The formation is effective because the returner doesn't know where the net player is going. That uncertainty can cause havoc in the recreational game because returners will often try to keep one eye on the net player as they prepare to hit the ball, resulting in frequent mishits and unforced errors.

The server lines up close to the center and hits almost all of her serves down the T. Keeping the ball in the middle of the court, cuts down on the returner's angles and can entice her to try to put too much on her shot.

As the net player, don't let the returner off the hook by making your move to soon. Wait until she commits to her return. If you move too early, not only do you take away the returner's anxiety over where you're going, but you open up the other half of the court.

Why not play this formation all the time? Primarily, because it requires a lot of effort and concentration. Every point is a poach point, so you and your partner expend a lot of energy. Additionally, a team that returns well will eventually begin to poke holes in it. Finally, it's easy to become predictable in your movements without even realizing it; when that happens, you lose the primary benefit of the formation.

Defending Against the I Formation

When your opponents set up in the I Formation, in which they line up one in front of the other down the center of the court, they are trying to disrupt your return game.

Don't get flustered. Instead, take a deep breath and take a step or two back from your normal return position.

The strength of the I Formation is the uncertainty it causes for the returner. You don't know in which direction the net player is going to move, and in an effort to outguess her, you make unforced errors or hit weak returns.

By stepping back, you force the net player to wait just that much longer before making her move. In the recreational game, most net players aren't that patient. She'll often give away her intention and then all you need to do is hit to the other side.

If your opponent doesn't move early, your best option is to drive the ball down the center of the court. Both opponents will often be leaning away from the middle, so their momentum will carry them away from your shot.

An added benefit of returning serve down the middle is, as the match progresses, the net player may start hesitating in the center, freeing you up to hit your cross-court returns again.

Always Defer the Serve

If you win the spin of the racquet at the beginning of the match, let your opponents serve first.

This choice has no downside.

What is their best outcome if they serve first? They win their serve, which they're supposed to do, so the best they can do is break even

What do you gain by letting them serve first?

Their first service game is your best opportunity to break, because the server won't be fully warmed up and into the match. Breaking early gives you an advantage that can set the tone for the rest of the match.

That means, of course, that you need to be laser-focused with the first point. Commit to getting back every return. Keep as much pressure on your opponents as you can. Don't give away any points. Make them win their serve.

If you break their serve, great. If not, it's your serve.

Of course, the odds are 50-50 that you'll lose the racquet spin. In most cases, though, your opponent will choose to serve first, so you benefit either way.

Get Your First Serve In

The serve plays an outsized role in doubles. About 30 percent of all shots in doubles are serves, and they account for 20 percent of all winning shots. Holding serve throughout the match makes your team hard to beat, while getting broken frequently—or struggling through every service game—makes it tough to come out on top.

The serving team has a significant advantage in doubles. By starting each point, you have the first chance to win the point or to put your opponents on the defensive.

Above all else, get your first serve in. Over the course of an average doubles match, you are two times more likely to win points on your first serve than on your second serve, because while returners tend to be defensive on first serves, they become more aggressive on second serves.

The primary reason recreational tennis players miss first serves is they try to hit the ball harder than they are capable, blasting rocket after rocket with 33 percent accuracy. If you're hitting a second serve on two out of every three points, you're proving the tired tennis truism that "You're only as good as your second serve."

Ratchet back the power on your first serve to three-quarters and aim to get seven out of ten serves in.

The best way to put some bite on a ¾ serve is to put some spin on the ball. Hitting with sidespin or topspin makes it more difficult for the receiver to tee off on the ball. Recreational players often step back to hit a spinning serve rather than attack it.

Additionally, a slower, spinning serve gives you time to get closer to the net for your first volley. That can mean the difference between punching your volley from above the top of the net and having to reach down to pick up a dipping ball at the service line.

Putting depth on your serve protects your partner at the net. A short serve comes back quickly, handcuffing your partner and forcing her to be more defensive. A deep topspin serve gives your partner more time to react to the ball and also limits the returner's shot choices.

Did I mention that you need to get your first serve in?

Serve Down The Middle

When serving to the deuce court (against a right-handed player) hit eight out of ten serves down the middle. Not only are you targeting the receiver's backhand, which is most players' weaker side, but you narrow the returner's angle of reply to the center of the court. As a result, your partner can cheat toward the middle, improving her poaching effectiveness.

The only reason to hit wide occasionally to the deuce court is to keep the receiver honest. Otherwise you're just hitting to her stronger side and widening her angle of reply. A better way to mix up your service game is to serve into the returner's body. You can often force a weak return.

In the ad court, you have the option of serving down the middle or wide. The down-the-middle serve gives your opponent a forehand return, but she is hitting into the strength of your formation. Serving wide gives the returner more angles, but most recreational players are hard-pressed to hit a penetrating return off their backhand.

If your partner has signaled her intention to poach, you must serve down the middle.

Adapt your service strategy as the match progresses. If, for example, the opponent in the deuce court is ripping her backhand returns, hit more serves into her body or test her wide forehand. Vary your serves until you find a strategy that works.

Keep Your Serving Options Open

Often in recreational doubles the server sets up as wide as she can, all the way out by the singles sideline. From here, she can hit her serve as wide as possible. Unfortunately, that's about all she can do.

Setting up wide is a good occasional tactic, but for several reasons, your team is better off if you start closer to the center of the court and hit most of your serves down the T.

Setting up wide narrows your angles, dictating where you're going to serve. The returner will set up wider because that's likely where you're going to serve, but even if you try to hit down the middle, the angle and spin on the ball will carry it toward the returner.

Serving wide also puts your partner under a lot of pressure because the returner has a larger angle of reply. She has a bigger margin for error going down the line and a better angle to hit a tight, cross-court return. Having to defend across such a broad front, your partner won't pose much of a poaching threat.

And you too are out of position. If your partner poaches, you'll be scrambling to reach anything hit down the line. And if the returner hits a tight-angled cross-court return, you will be hard-pressed to put much on your volley.

If you still want to set up wide, do it almost exclusively to the ad court against righties or the deuce court against lefties, because at least you'll be targeting their backhands.

The First Volley

In recreational tennis, serving and volleying is often a reluctant strategy. A lot of us aren't skilled, practiced, or confident enough to hit a penetrating serve, move into the court, and hit that first volley from around the service line with pace and placement.

If you are more likely to miss your first serve due to the pressure of having to follow it in, or if your volley is more likely to end up at the bottom of the net, don't feel that you must serve and volley. The whole point of strategic doubles is to keep the ball in play and if you're winning more points by serving and staying back, do that.

Still, make serving and volleying your goal. No single tactic in the game is as important as taking control of the net. Eighty percent of winners during the run of play are at the net. The serve and volley can be divided into three phases: Serve, approach, and volley.

The best serve is deep, spinning, 3/4-speed, and hit down the middle. Serving deep and at 3/4-speed gives you time to move into the court. Putting spin on the ball prevents your opponent from setting up and teeing off on the ball. Hitting down the middle limits the returner's angles; you and your partner will be well placed to volley back most returns. An occasional serve out wide will keep the returners on their toes.

When you come in behind your serve, be prepared to hit every ball. It's a safe bet. About 85 percent of all service returns are hit cross-court.

After serving, move forward as far as you can before stopping and preparing to respond to the return. Some players have a set number of steps they take, such as three or four. Others try to reach a specific point on the court, such as the service line. And still others time their movement to the serve, split-stepping when their serve lands in the court. Find the method that works for you, but make sure you have stopped moving forward before the returner strikes the ball.

The farther forward you can get the better. This first volley is the most difficult one in the game because you're farther away from the net. At the same time, it is the most important volley, because more than half of all points won by the returning team come from mishit first volleys by the server. Focus on putting your volley in the court and as deep as possible.

Rather than follow the direction of your serve to the net, approach down the middle of your side of the court. You'll be able to cover the returner's shots. As the match progresses, you will get a sense for your opponents' return patterns and can adapt your movement.

Base your volley placement on which side of your body you're hitting from. If it's an outside return (the ball is between you and the sideline), you need to get the ball past the opposing net player, so hit a sharp-angled volley cross-court. If the net player is an aggressive poacher, an occasional volley down the line will keep her honest.

On inside returns (the ball is between you and the center line), your best volley is down the middle. In most instances the net player won't have a play on the ball, so focus on keeping the ball deep.

One caveat: One of the best replies to serving and volleying is the lob return over your partner's head. Because you are the deeper player and the crosscourt player, that ball is your responsibility. So even as all of your momentum is pushing you toward the net, you have to stop, change direction, and retrieve the lob. Fortunately, recreational players don't hit the lob return too often.

Get the Return Back

First, the bad news. The returning team in a typical doubles match loses twice as many points as it wins. According to match statistics, only about 10 percent of service returns are winners, around 40 percent are outright errors, and the remainder face the gauntlet of the opposing net player and the onrushing server.

Now the good news. If you get your return back over the net, your team's chances of winning the point climb to almost 50/50. In fact, most points won by the return team are on the initial return—often by forcing an error on the server's first volley.

And even better news. If the server doesn't come in behind her serve and you follow your return into the net, you flip the odds of winning the point from two-to-one against to two-to-one for.

So…get the return back. You can't win the point if you don't return the serve. Remember, you're playing recreational doubles, in which even the most lame-duck return can result in an unforced error..

Decide before the point where you are going to hit your return. It can be different depending on whether the serve comes to your forehand or backhand. Ignore the movement of both the net player and the server. Don't go for a winner; focus on the ball.

Hit the majority of your returns cross-court.

Unless the server stays back every time, assume she's coming in behind her serve. Ideally, you'll hit a low return to make the server's first volley as difficult as possible, but your first imperative is to get the ball back, so hit the ball high enough to consistently clear the net.

The angled cross-court dink works best off the backhand. It's a sliced, under-spinning shot that lands short in the service box and bounces low. It's a difficult ball for the server to pick off on her first volley because she has to bend down and hit it from below the top of the net.

On the forehand side, the topspin drive works well because you can put some power behind it—making a poach more difficult—and it gets to the server faster, forcing her to hit her first volley farther away from the net.

Against really difficult serves, lob your returns over the net player's head.

When facing a second serve, move in a couple of paces, because you can expect a more conservative serve. On serves that land short, or if the server stays back, follow your return to the net.

Always look to move forward to take the net. It is the single most important move the returning team can make to have the best chance to win the game.

If the server doesn't come in behind her serve, whether on the first or second serve, move forward on your return—regardless of the quality of your return.

When Your Partner is Serving

When your partner is serving, position yourself about halfway between the net and the service line and about one or two feet inside the center line. If you feel confident about your volley, move a step or two closer in. As the match plays out, adjust your starting position based on your opponents' skills and return patterns.

Prior to and during the serve, you want to distract the returner as much as you can within the rules. "Within the rules" is the key phrase. What constitutes a hindrance is vague. Suffice it to say that it's a lot like pornography—you know it when you see it.

One of the best ways to carve out a thick slice of the returner's concentration is to fake the poach. The key to a successful fake is moving early enough that you can affect the return. As the returner is setting up, step toward the middle as if you are poaching and then, once she's committed to her shot, move back into position.

Vary where you set up in the forecourt. Always position yourself so you can protect your side of the court, but even a slight change in your set-up can cause a small tear in your opponent's concentration.

If you have communicated to your partner that you're going to poach, you must poach. Don't hold off moving until the last moment to try to catch your opponent by surprise. Your responsibility is to cover the cross-court return. If you wait to move, you won't be able to do that. Don't worry about the returner hitting behind you; your partner has that side of the court covered.

If the poach isn't on, focus on the returner. Even though you and your partner will have communicated the direction of the serve prior to the point starting, intent doesn't always match reality, so watch which way the returner moves.

If it's an inside serve—closer to the center line—take a diagonal step forward and toward the center strap. You are now in a good position to cut off most cross-court returns, while still being able to defend your side of the court.

If it's an outside serve—closer to the sideline—move a step forward. Although there is a tendency to want to protect the alley against a down-the-line shot, your opponent's more dangerous return remains cross-court, so focus on that shot. Hitting down-the-line is not a high percentage return, so luring the returner to try to thread the needle can be a good match strategy.

On second serves, most returners will step up and slap a powerful return—often directed right at you. Set up a couple of feet farther back and one or two paces closer to the middle of the service box and prepare to defend your court.

If your partner has a weak second serve or your opponent has a savage return game, move back towards or even at the baseline. Don't stick with a formation that should work, but doesn't.

Occasionally, you will encounter an opponent—or opponents—who have grooved their down-the-line return. If they keep winning points with it, take away that option.

When Your Partner is Returning

When your partner is returning serve and you're at the net, start every point with the same progression.

Set up a few paces in front of the service line. This position gives you the widest range of options during the first few shots of each point.

Focus on the opposing net player rather than the serve. If she moves to poach your partner's service return, hold your position and prepare to make a defensive volley. In most instances, the poacher will volley to your feet. Even though you are in an exposed position, unless she hits the ball cleanly, you may still have a play on the ball.

If the opposing net player stays put, turn your attention to the server.

If she's coming in behind her serve, base your play on her movements. If she goes to hit a high volley, she has a wide range of targets and you make a tempting one—so be prepared.

If she moves to hit a low volley from below the net, move forward and diagonally toward the center strap. She will have to volley the ball up and you may be able to cut it off.

If the server stays back, move forward a couple of paces.

One important note: In recreational tennis, you will often see the net player calling the service line for her partner. This is a big Don't. If you're watching the serve, you are not concentrating on the opposing net player, who must be your focus at the beginning of every point.

Fixing a Losing Game

When you're on the wrong end of the score, ask yourselves the question: "Are we losing or are they winning?" The answer determines your strategy.

If you're losing the match, it's probably because you're making too many unforced errors. Unfortunately, when on the wrong side of the score, most of us try to hit the ball even harder and go for even more winners, which as you may have guessed, is the absolutely wrong thing to do.

Your better option is for your partner and you to focus on keeping the ball in play.

Spin in your serve to increase your service percentage.

Chip your service returns to increase your net clearance.

Hit down the center of the court.

Take pace and depth off your volleys to keep them in the court

Lob more often—even on service returns.

By playing longer points, you have more of a chance to find your rhythm and you give your opponents more of an opportunity to make an error.

If you are playing well, but your opponents are outplaying you, turn your focus on their game. What are they doing well, and more importantly, is there something they aren't doing well? Once you uncover a weakness—no matter how small—attack it.

A lot of recreational players, for example, are really good at returning pace with pace. Rather than giving them a steady diet of hard-hit balls, take something off your shots and inject some slice.

Changing your serving formation can disrupt your opponents' return game. The I Formation—in which the server and net player line up in an I along the center line and the net player poaches only after the returner has committed to her shot—is particularly effective against opponents who are cutting you open with their service returns. If one of your opponents has a potent cross-court return, use the Australian Formation—in which the net player sets up on the same side of the court as the server.

Predictability can be a trap. While you want to hit your best shots, sometimes you unwittingly get into a rut and rely on the same shots in the same situations. Mixing up your game—without messing it up—can prevent your opponents from anticipating your shots.

The Set-Up Volley

Match statistics show that the deep volley is the most lethal stroke during the run of play in doubles. By an almost two-to-one margin, it accounts for the most winners in a match.

Statistics, however, don't tell the whole story.

One of the primary reasons why the deep volley is so deadly is that it is often preceded by the short angled volley that opens up your opponents' formation.

The keys to the set-up volley are to hit the ball as softly and as tightly angled to the net as you can. In most instances you're not going to hit a winner on this shot, so keep the ball inside the service box; don't flirt with the sideline. Your goal is to force your opponents to have to hit up on the ball, giving your partner or you the opportunity to step in and strike the deep volley.

Whenever you have to hit a volley from below the level of the net, cross-court is your best—only?—option. Hitting straight ahead, you need to put more air under the ball to clear the net, giving your opponents the opportunity to hit down on their volley.

If you can meet the ball above the net, hit the angled volley with a more pace. It may not be an immediate winner, but you will likely shred your opponents' formation.

When you hit the soft angled volley, both you and your partner need to slide in the direction of the shot. Your opponent's best response is to hit the ball back across the center strap, so you want to be positioned to cut off the shot and hit a hard, crisp volley deep into the space that she had to vacate to reach your set-up volley.

Ten Quick Tips

Watch the Ball. Those three words have been an admonishment since the first-ever tennis lesson, but the instruction is even more important in doubles, because you have so much more competing for your attention. Ignore the movement of the server and the net player. Focus on the ball.

Get Your First Serve In. One of the biggest predictors of match success in recreational doubles is a high first serve percentage. If you get your first serve in—and follow it in to the net—you are likely to win as many as eight out of ten of your service points. Missing too many first serves, on the other hand, makes it easier for your opponents to take the offensive and capture the net.

Decide Early Where You're Going to Hit Your Shot. Don't try to figure out what your opponents are going to do as you're hitting the ball. In any given situation in doubles, there's the proper shot to hit. Decide on it early and commit to it.

Hit Where They Used To Be. If one of your opponents is constantly moving in the court, don't try to guess where she won't be. Hit the ball where she was. Not only do you have good odds that she won't still be there, but once she catches on to what you're doing, she'll stop moving so much.

Keep Moving Forward. Doubles is won at the net. Keep moving forward. All the time. On every shot. If you get lobbed and are forced back to the baseline, start moving forward again.

Poach More Often. Most recreational players don't poach enough. We're so concerned with protecting our side of the court that we don't attack poachable balls. If you and your partner are on the same page, she will cover for you as you poach, so poach more often.

Fake Poach More Often. Faking the poach can be almost as effective as poaching. In recreational doubles, players will often try to adjust their shot when they see you move at the net, resulting in an unforced error or a ball hit right back at you.

Aim at the Net Player's Feet. Any time you volley the ball from above the top of the net, hit at the net player's feet. Even if she can manufacture a return, she won't be able to put anything on it.

Be Patient. There's always an urge to get the point over with quickly, to blast the ball past your opponents or to go for the high-risk placement. Ignore that urge. Focus instead on hitting the right shots at the right time. This strategy will force "unforced" errors from your opponents or give you a put-away shot.

Communicate Strategically. While a lot of the communication between doubles partners is to maintain a connection and to keep up morale, it's also vital to talk strategy before and after points. If you spot a weakness in one of your opponents—a tendency to hit a short second serve, slow feet, constantly hitting the same shot in the same situation or difficulty handling certain shots—point it out to your partner and make sure both of you take advantage of it

And one more....

Lob More Often. Recreational players don't lob enough. Lob more on the return of serve, lob more when you're pulled off the court, lob more when you're opponents are pressing forward, lob more when they are hitting overheads. Lob more.

Printed in Great Britain
by Amazon